Fire Trucks

Kate Riggs

CREATIVE EDUCATION • CREATIVE PAPERBACKS

seedlings

Published by Creative Education and Creative Paperbacks
P.O. Box 227, Mankato, Minnesota 56002
Creative Education and Creative Paperbacks
are imprints of The Creative Company
www.thecreativecompany.us

Design by Ellen Huber
Production by Travis Green
Art direction by Rita Marshall
Printed in Malaysia

Photographs by Alamy (David R. Frazier Photolibrary, Inc.),
Corbis (Hans Gutknecht/ZUMA Press, Transtock), Dreamstime
(Le-thuy Do, Aaron Johnson, Wendy Kaveney, Tyler Olson,
Ulrich Mueller, Thomas Perkins, Satori13, Ron Zmiri), Getty
Images (Andy Caulfield, Gilles Mingasson, Simone Mueller,
Bob Peterson), iStockphoto (ryasick, yzak), Shutterstock
(japape, Kesu, eileen meyer, Anita Patterson Peppers)

Library of Congress Cataloging-in-Publication Data
Riggs, Kate.
Fire trucks / Kate Riggs.
p. cm. — (Seedlings)
Includes bibliographical references and index.
Summary: A kindergarten-level introduction to fire trucks,
covering their firefighters, equipment, role in rescuing, and
such defining features as their ladders.
ISBN 978-1-60818-581-8 (hardcover)
IBSN 978-1-62832-186-9 (pbk)
1. Fire engines—Juvenile literature. I. Title.

TH9372.R54 2015
628.9'259—dc23   2014034718

CCSS: RI.K.1, 2, 3, 4, 5, 6, 7;
RI.1.1, 2, 3, 4, 5, 6, 7; RF.K.1, 3; RF.1.1

First Edition HC 9 8 7 6 5 4 3 2 1
First Edition PBK 9 8 7 6 5 4 3 2 1

TABLE OF CONTENTS

Time to help!

Fire trucks help put out fires.

They save people and animals.

Fire trucks are big, long vehicles. Many are red and white. Some are yellow.

A fast fire truck has flashing lights. It uses sirens to let people know it is coming.

On top of a fire truck is a ladder. It can reach high into the air.

Hoses are inside the truck.

One firefighter
drives the truck.
Other firefighters
hook up the hoses
to water.

When the fire is gone, the truck goes back to the station. Firefighters wash the truck. They put away their gear.

Ready to help again!

Picture a Fire Truck

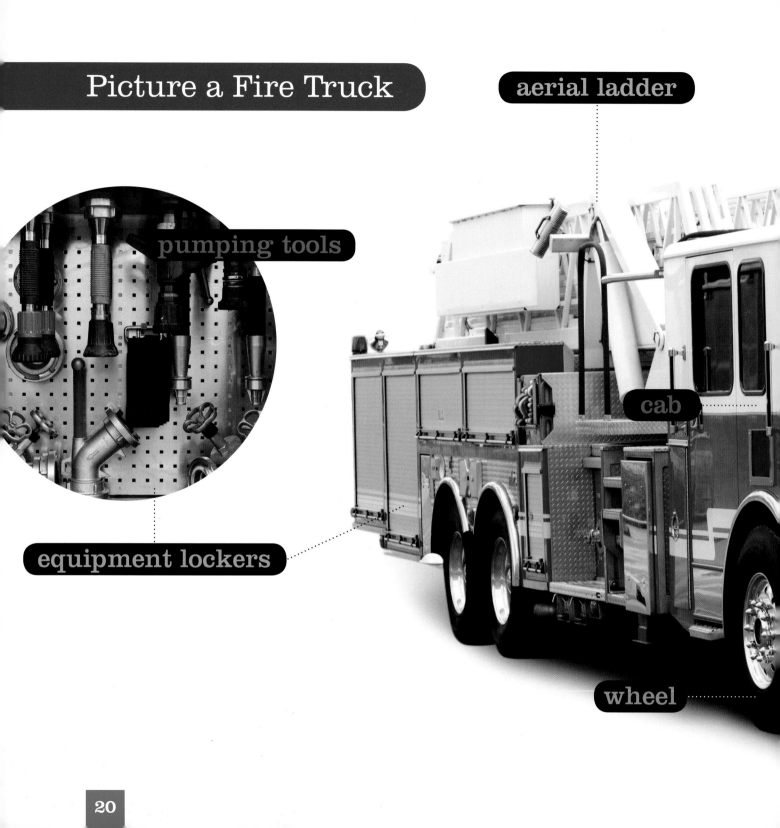

aerial ladder

pumping tools

cab

equipment lockers

wheel

emergency light

siren

Words to Know

sirens: things that make loud noises as a sign that a vehicle is coming

station: the place where fire trucks are parked

Read More

Chancellor, Deborah. *Fire Rescue.*
Mankato, Minn.: Smart Apple Media, 2014.

Lindeen, Mary. *Fire Trucks.*
Minneapolis: Bellwether Media, 2007.

Websites

DLTK's Fire Truck Craft
http://www.dltk-kids.com/crafts/miscellaneous
/egg_carton_fire_truck.htm
Make your own fire truck out of an egg carton.

Fire Safe Kids Coloring Pages
http://www.firesafekids.org/coloring.html
Print out firefighter pages to color, and play fire safety games.

Note: Every effort has been made to ensure that the websites listed above are suitable for children, that they have educational value, and that they contain no inappropriate material. However, because of the nature of the Internet, it is impossible to guarantee that these sites will remain active indefinitely or that their contents will not be altered.

23

Index